THE SOUTHEAST ASIAN BOOK OF THE DEAD

By
Bill Shields

©1993 2.13.61 Publications

SECOND PRINTING

D1340115

Cov

Layout & design by **Endless Graphics**

2.13.61
P.O. BOX 1910 · LOS ANGELES ·
CALIFORNIA · 90078 · USA

2.13.61 INFO HOTLINE #: (213)969-8043

Other books from 2.13.61:

FOREWORD

by HUBERT SELBY, JR.

The first thing I noticed about Bill Shields new book is the progression of his writing. There is an increasing confidence in his "ear" and the ability to get what he "hears" on the paper. He knows what he wants from each line, and how to achieve it. The rhythms are clear and distinct, the "beat" inherent. He obviously is very comfortable in bringing each poem to its appropriate emphasis with a declining line, the crescendo peaking in the penultimate line and quietly resolving itself with a deceptively quiet final, short, line, usually a simple word or two.

The book is, to my ear and eye, a mans search for himself through a previous generation and the following generation, a search where he sees himself being a conduit for the poison of the past to the future, a future he dreads, perhaps, even more than his own present (presence). His days, nights, awake, asleep, are haunted by the horrors of Vietnam, yet the horrors are almost a comfort for him as he views himself as a monster and harbinger of death even without his history in that war; a tortured mind, and scarred psyche, trying to find the cause of his present horror in the jungles of Vietnam, yet finding more relief in that horror than freedom from it would afford. A man who inwardly tries to view himself as a victim of the war, the battleground of that war, but in his inner-most self believes he is the war, and the war is his only escape from himself and the demon that haunts and tortures him, and so the dead and mutilated bodies, his constant companions, are his only source of comfort. He longs to join them but can not find the means. No matter how many gun barrels he sucks on he can't make the trip and toss his own hated and hateful body, and mind, on the pile of broken bones and rotted flesh.

This is a tortured book, written by a tortured man (mind), who is trying to find, and free, himself in, and by, his writing, a man who is the battleground of the Hounds of Heaven and the Hounds of Hell, and he doesn't know which are which, and if he thinks he has finally found out they switch around on him and so he is eternally damned, and doomed.

This is a torturous book to read. Bill Shields has not spared himself, nor us. I can only hope that pounding the keys of his typewriter has helped him exorcise some of his demon, or at least to discover that he is NOT the demon.

THE SOUTHEAST ASIAN BOOK OF THE DEAD

For KATHLEEN

My thanks to Keith Dodson, Rod Sperry, Cathy Lynn, Ca Conrad, Cheryl Townsend, Elliot Richman, and Blacky Hix for their continuing support.

This book would not exist without the vision and encouragement of Henry Rollins.

BLOOD RAIN

The nights I walk around this apartment wishing bychrist the front door would swing wide & a man will walk in w/ metal jacketed rounds & put one right thru my right eye. I don't have the courage to do it myself but I have the desire.

My wife is sleeping w/a bruised throat & an alarm clock. I have taken her kindness & eaten her dry. She has lived w/my screams & nightmares about Vietnam for four years & there won't be many more. No, the end of this is coming, a matter-of-time.

I have no money, car payments, another ex-wife, & no excuses. My brother & sister haven't seen me in years; my father may or may not be alive. It doesn't matter.

My kids are in another state; they know my voice on the phone. Three alive. I buried one.

‡ ‡ ‡ ‡

I was a young man, 18 years old, before I saw my first dead body. Might as well been a carp, for all I felt, a carp w/one eye out & mutilated fins. A small girl in a nameless Vietnamese town, all of six homes & six fireplaces... everything coated in mud & war. A thin pig was chewing on her 2 leg, grunting as it tore into her.

The guy next to me had been in the Nam for five months. He killed the pig; we all ate it later & it tasted fine.

No spirit of a dead girl flew into us.

Just hog.

I tore off chunks.

‡ ‡ ‡ ‡

That whole year was death & mutilation; everywhere I looked there where bodies piled up, smeared in lime, waiting on the bulldozer. People in villages were missing arms & legs... burns from napalm.

No one ever wrote about war & described how the bodies farted & belched for hours after their demise, Yes. Hours of very human sounds come out of very dead bodies, & the rats that come to eat don't mind a bit. They'll eat good. I've seen w/my eyes bodies killed, laying on concertina wire for hours, & rats shaking their bones to pieces.

‡ ‡ ‡ ‡

I sat for days once, on a river bank, waiting to kill a man. I shit myself, I pissed myself, I waited. & the only thought I had was how bad I wanted a cigarette.

Every movement slow, exaggerated in its slowness, I shot the little bastard. The blood came out of his neck like water out of water pistol; he died bone innocent of me.

I sat a while longer, lighting up a Salem & smelling myself. It wasn't a bad moment.

‡ ‡ ‡ ‡

That image put me in the VA hospital for a couple months.

The bodies never stopped coming. I'd shoot one & another took his place; blood spurted out of fifty men's heads & into the filthy My Tho river. Fish boiled the surface, bathing themselves in human gore. I never stopped firing.

I was sitting on a couch in New Hampshire, sneaking out at night to get milk & etc. at the 7-11... I sat there for weeks, seeing bodies pile hundreds of feet high, popping caps at everything. Everything died. Personally.

‡ ‡ ‡ ‡

7

Even the fucking ground was dead. We'd ride patrol boats down brown rivers & see cracked, brown mud & swamp w/o vegetation for miles... hours. The occasional bush or tree would be all that was left in acres of mud & swamp.

No animals, no people. Dirt falling into an already filthy sewer.

It was a good place to be.

No one & I mean no one ever bitched about Agent Orange; I could've kissed Dow Chemical on its corporate ass. It trimmed the wings of that nasty ghost hummingbird: Mr. Charles. But it was damn sure strange to look at all those miles of the Sahara Desert in the middle of a jungle.

But if I had known that the defoliant was going to kill us, I'd have taken the Cong on w/o a weapon & a mouthful of spit.

When my own daughter died from my exposure to Agent Orange, I did load up weapons into my Escort & lit for the corporate headquarters of Dow & Death.

& that's another story.

≠ ≠ ≠ ≠

Heads on a pole, heads on a pole, heads on a pole - it got rhythm, as close to hell as you can get.

The head shrinks a little w/o a body.

I shrunk before it, stuck on a bamboo shoot, staring at it for minutes; my mind switched off, totally numb to my eyes. I went quietly insane before it, way beyond horror, beyond mutilation; my buddy, Bill Quackenbush, stuck a cigarette in its mouth & took a 35 mm picture w/his new Yashica. Other guys posed w/ it, pictures all around.

We left it there. The maggots had already found it, crawling thru its ears. No one would touch it - the scalp already starting to lift from the head.

Walk on, Trooper.

‡ ‡ ‡ ‡

It was when I was first married & children were crawling the rug; my oldest daughter on my lap as I rocked her to sleep in the front room of our rented trailer... my wife was a ghost of a woman, the kids sucking the soul right out of her body. She must've been asleep at the time.

I took that child of mine & a .44 under the trailer w/the bugs & spiders. Actually dragged an old air mattress under there & some kid's toys. Candybars & Kool-Aid. It was the most secure place I had had since Can Tho city, looking thru the mobile home skirting. A loaded .44 & a child that depended on me I had it down stone cold.

My in-laws came a few months later & took the kids & took the wife; I hated them. Americans w/no scars swinging the flag. Every asshole got the same wrinkles.

‡ ‡ ‡ ‡

Jim Davidson was a fool.

We were doing a sweep of a village, about twenty of us circling around some hootches, walking in w/weapons set on maximum rock & roll; the light was fading & steam was heavy on the jungle floor... this little kid came running at us... we screamed for him to stop, goddamnit stop! & he kept on, heading for Davidson, who was screaming w/the rest of us.

The kid ran right on top of him & pulled the satchel charge on his back, blowing Davidson into the weeds in pieces.

I don't know why we never killed that kid.

‡ ‡ ‡ ‡

Her legs were curled behind her in an old, old chair, a dog at her feet & a glass of Tang on the small table.

She had been steadily vomiting blood & vodka into a towel for an hour; the ashtray was filled w/Camels floating in her stomach acid.

I walked over & gave her a kiss on the cheek & said:

Mom.

╪ ╪ ╪ ╪

A small room w/curtains separating five beds. Men snarling motherfucker/whore/slut/cunt/slope/gook cunt... a fist connecting w/a whore's face. You paid your money, you took your whore.

I was on my side looking at this woman, no more than 16 years old, & bad dead to any emotion; we were a good pair, a couple.

Her arms abscessed from heroin, nasty nasty pus sores & red streaks running up her arms. Poppy eyes. She hadn't felt the last hundred men that jumped her 4'10" frame. I don't think she even knew she was pregnant.

╪ ╪ ╪ ╪

He was going to die if I didn't cut his throat w/ a Bowie knife.

We were in a helicopter coming back from a mission that failed deep in blood; guys gut wounded screaming above the sounds of the helo blades; I slipped once on the sandbags on the floor, so coated in blood, I was walking on ice 1000 feet in the air. Morphine syrettes all around... battle dressings already soaked clear thru in blood.

& one guy turning blue, holding his head. A round had gone right thru his face, broken his jaw & shot the teeth right out of him. His tongue blown off & laying in his airway. No air, no life.

I cut him asshole-to-elbow & stuck a piece of surgical tubing in his throat... a fancy tracheotomy. His color got better before he fainted.

Mine never got better.

╫╫╫╫

Couple nights ago I was dead, locked in tight w/the arms of war, asleep on my bed here in Youngwood PA. The firefights are always more vivid, more precise in their brilliance... the bone chips of the Viet Cong damn near glow in my walls.

I felt cold steel on my left eye, a strong pressure & a smell of gun oil.

My wife had straddled me, pinning my legs to the bed & a gun to my head. I never saw her face, it was so black. I didn't struggle.

The words came from the grave: No more, Bill Shields, no more, & she pulled the trigger.

Of course, I died.

I feel no different.

╫╫╫╫

The last five minutes of my first marriage were 6:30 to 6:35 a.m. on the edge of a snowbank. My ex-wife screaming at me not to come back w/o a refrigerator & I didn't.

╫╫╫╫

They never heard a damn thing; we slithered into the hootch & put a round into the old man's head w/o even his wife stirring next to him.

On the way out, I rigged a white phosphorus grenade to the door - letting it hang on monofilament line - so when they woke up in the morning & opened the door, the grenade would detonate.

They'd burn to death. They did burn to death.

We went back a couple days later to see how they were.

†††

A dead Amerasian baby floating down the My Tho river... I was on a barge, stuck right in the middle of the river, sipping a coke & watching the sunrise. The guy on watch shared a joint w/me; we were listening to an eight-track tape of the Jefferson Airplane, wishing to christ we were back home getting our share of that free love & dope.

That baby ran into the piling, then the current took the body downstream. Those tiny blue eyes were looking straight into hell.

†††

He had sat next to me in a veteran's rap group for six months, a big bear of a guy barely thirty yet married twice w/three kids. He talked less than me - I liked him. So many of the guys sitting there loved to talk about the Nam, missing the adrenaline & the firepower... men stuck forever at a point in their life, gauging everything to one experience. Hell, I'm guilty of that too. But I was quiet, so was this guy.

The VA let him out of the violent lockup ward once a week for meetings. He had tried to strangle his wife & child one night, mistaking them in the dark for Vietnamese.

I understood that - done it myself.

He was an okay guy.

†††

My father had been drinking & spitting our teeth for days; our mother was gone, off to see her parents, & the old man had been carrying a bottle w/him since.
He took a swing at my little brother - he must've been six at the

time - & that small boy threw an ashtray at the old man's mouth, meeting teeth & lips.

If that man is still alive, he's carrying those scars.

My brother grew up to be a computer programmer who drives an old Ford & blames his fucked life on his own kids.

‡ ‡ ‡ ‡

200,000 prostitutes.
879,000 orphans.
181,000 disabled.
1,000,000 widows.
19,000,000 tons of herbicide sprayed.
1,500,000 farm animals killed.
9,000 hamlets destroyed.
Vietnam.

‡ ‡ ‡ ‡

I came home to Western Pennsylvania in the middle of snow & freezing rain; 2 days before I had been loaded into a plane in Saigon, flipped the bird against the window & sweated in the air-conditioning. Took 3 Darvon, rushed 'em down w/coffee. Stopped in Hawaii, stopped in San Francisco, where they missed finding the pot I was bringing home. Caught a commercial flight to Pittsburgh, then caught a commuter flight to my home town. 11 p.m. Only passenger.

I didn't have a coat & the terminal was closed. I popped the bottle of Darvon: 3 more. Washed those bad boys down dry.

The headlights of that Dodge Dart were slow in coming; maybe I waited half an hour, maybe longer, standing under the roof of that little airport lounge. A 4 cigarette wait. Bad shakes for a boy acclimated to 100 degree jungle.

They showed. My brother grinned from the wheel:
"Didn' think we was going to leave you here alone, eh fucker?"

13

My mother passed me back a beer.

┊ ┊ ┊

I spent that first night home, alone in the livingroom; the lights turned off, watching tv & sipping coke, munching chips. The family dog sniffed all the Vietnam off me. I fell asleep on the couch.

My brother took a pound of my pot & disappeared to a friend's house; my mother went to her room.

I woke up in the basement, crouched in the corner by the clothes chute - my knife out, listening for movement, a rush in the dark. I almost killed that damn dog & he didn't even know it.

I cried for myself down there in the dirty clothes; yes I did, furious that this was what I came home to. Nothing but myself.

┊ ┊ ┊

The third time I splintered the door w/my knife my mother drove me into Pittsburgh, the VA Hospital, where they prescribed Thorazine to keep me calm enough to finish out my 30 day leave & return to the Navy.

I hadn't been home for 72 hours before someone tried to sedate me & succeeded.

┊ ┊ ┊

I found my Purple Hearts the day after we buried my mother. We were cleaning out her dresser & they were in her jewelry box - thrown in like a bad thought, crumpled next to her wedding band. They had been there for nine years, lost.

There were letters tucked in the bottom of the box, love letters from a guy she was engaged to in WW II, & a newspaper clipping of his death in France. He hadn't been a hero, just a grunt eating metal.

I threw it all away, stuck the whole mess of that dresser under-wear, sweaters, pants, & memorabilia - all of it in the trash. Purple Hearts too. & a 1/2 filled bottle of Gilbey's. My sister took the rings.

‡ ‡ ‡ ‡

He had been 15 feet away & just plain evaporated into a red fog, a blood rain. Caught a rocket square in the chops.

Somebody had lied to the boy; I know John Wayne lied to him. I know Kennedy lied to him. I know he lied to himself, playing a stupid hero, when all that gets anyone is dead.

I pulled a sliver of his bone out of my face. That was the biggest piece of Serge LaRiviere we ever found.

His mother got a flag.

He's probably still sitting on top of the tv at home, a nice frame around the picture.

‡ ‡ ‡ ‡

My first memory of childhood is a wounded rabbit that our family cat dragged in the kitchen; that alley cat had a grip on its neck that no man could shake. The bunny cried like a child & died by the stove. I stood w/the family & watched it. There was so little else to do.

‡ ‡ ‡ ‡

No one ever spat on me.

But I didn't wear my uniform much.

My sister didn't speak to me till 1975. She became a public accountant & forgot she ever slept w/a black man, danced at a love-in, & hated the Vietnam war. She married an attorney, had two kids & a Volvo. She consumed her life.

‡ ‡ ‡ ‡

I married her in Rockville Maryland, pronounced guilty by a justice of the peace; hell no, I didn't love her, & I didn't love myself but I did feel the need for a round-eyed woman w/ brunette hips. I takes five minutes to get married & a lifetime to get their voice out of your ear.

She came from a shithole in Minnesota w/abusive parents; I was going to be more of the same.

The honeymoon lasted five days at a Motel Six in Jacksonville Florida; she left for home. I stayed w/the Navy.

I'm still sending checks for those damn kids.

‡ ‡ ‡

I totally fucked my first killing, a side of beef hanging at the grocery store is carved w/more finesse.

The team had walked from the river, a good two blind black miles thru jungle, onto this village that was tucked between paddies. Hard core Viet Cong ville, total commitment. A quiet town at 2:15 a.m.

I caught movement to my right, about 100 feet from the nearest hootch, & I smelled him. He was cautious, noise disciplined, walking his perimeter. I stalked him slow, downwind.

& I came up on top of him, my knife slipping off the back of his head, stabbing him in the shoulder. My hand was in his mouth, cutting off a scream, & I stuck him again, ripping his entire throat open. Hardcore cat, he fought me down; I was on my knees when the knife went in perfectly, right in the back of the head.

I was coated in his blood & the bugs ate me alive; it was the first spinal cord I ever saw.

‡ ‡ ‡

Two weeks before she died, I carried my mother out of a restaurant bathroom; she had passed out on the pot, ice-cold, I thought she was dead. She pulled her head up, out of her chest saying of-course-I'm-alright & I carried her out.

When she passed out again at the table, we ate our meal as she slept w/her mouth open.

She had her chance.

‡ ‡ ‡

Rochester Minnesota. A town w/ boarding houses & chemo-therapy patients walking the streets. Mayo Clinic. You come there when your only other option is the grave.

I pulled my daughter out of a children's hospital in Minneapolis, packed her in the car on a Sunday afternoon with plenty of blankets. Wind chill of 75 degrees below hell. I held her forty pounds & drove.

She lasted four days on the pediatric oncology ward. The leukemia won on a Wednesday & she died holding my hand.

I left town w/three days left on the room.

‡ ‡ ‡

I can be such an asshole: I came out of the shower, raging inside, thinking of my past & the fools who've inhabited my body, & I broke the shower rod & smashed the mirror w/my hand. I heard the door slam shut - my wife has been thru this many times before. Just a stupid moment. I have many.

‡ ‡ ‡

NO AMERICANS BEYOND THIS POINT - that's what the sign said, a beat up sheet of plywood hanging across the river between Vietnam & Cambodia.

You are now entering Cambodia.

Death doesn't care where you fall; its hands are always open.

‡ ‡ ‡ ‡

I like the anonymity of a pancake house, sitting alone for hours under bright fluorescent tubes, sipping out of a bottomless cup. My clothes have stuck to a lot of booths.

No one has ever asked for my name.

‡ ‡ ‡ ‡

Five of us joined the service right out of high school: 2 in the marines, 2 in the army, me in the navy. 1969.

Bill Strickler died at the siege of Con Thien; Timmy Dolde died in the Iron Triangle; Big Jim Schomer killed himself in a rented room, the needle still in his arm; Ed Schomer, the badass Green Beret, died in 1982 of 6 different cancers that ate his brain & his bones. Not one of us survived.

‡ ‡ ‡ ‡

Not one bit of romance in a small room, a writer cutting his/her wrists for the goddamn words as the cockroaches fuck in the soup bowls. Bukowski is wrong.

A bed on the floor, a typewriter on the landlord's table, 2 pairs of pants, 4 shirts, a couple shoes, books & a boom box. That's all I owned, everything. Nothing

I've lived to slam the keyboard; the words saved my life when there was no, absolutely no reason to wake up in the morning. I'd fall asleep on the floor trying to believe in a god enough for him to take my life. In the morning, I'd mail out poetry submissions. The first magazine that published me - MURDER'S WORK - I stuck on the wall; it was horrible but my words were buried in it.

I'd go work in the morning at a print shop, work the eight out & catch the bus home at night. A bowl of Campbell's & a sandwich. Fight the rage & the guilt, make the words better than a movie, better than a picture.

Years. Many typewriters.

I'm still doing it, busting this whore word processor against the fucking wall when the words leave me; it's all that matters, the words.

‡ ‡ ‡ ‡

I never felt my finger being ripped off my hand. We were in grass 6 feet high, laying in the swamp mud as a full platoon of Viet Cong were leapfrogging us, going from one body to the next, sticking them w/a bayonet. On our backs, a .45 in one hand & a knife in the other.

Screams from the wounded; the Viet Cong broke noise discipline talking to each other, confident they had us dead & our bodies stripped. A flash of black pants & another man would scream. I heard one asshole laughing w/his pal as they moved to my position.

I waited, urine running down my leg, my hand shaking the .45 wildly; they came behind me, quiet then as snakes, & the youngest shot a round at me, hitting my hand as the older gentleman jabbed a bayonet at my face. I shot the young man right in the goddamn head, he was never going to see his sixteenth birthday; the old man flat slithered away.

We went in there w/10 men. Five men came out wounded, carrying five dead.

‡ ‡ ‡ ‡

I loaded a M-14, 2 white phosphorous grenades, a Browning automatic shotgun, a Ruger .44 magnum, & 2.2 pounds of C4 plastics into my Ford Escort. Ammunition went in the back seat, covered over by my daughter's blanket. A Visa card & a Rand McNally map. I wasn't planning on living long enough for a

19

change of clothes. My daughter had been dead only a few days; I was going to kill any one directly involved w/developing Agent Orange at Dow Chemical, methodically spraying the lab walls w/their body parts. No more reasons, no more excuses; the greyhound busline to hell was on time & I was driving w/both hands on the wheel.

Called my ex-wife from the road, outside of Madison Wisconsin, apologized for ever being a father. She said nothing. I was right.

I drove for days not reading the map, charging gas at every small town station that took a credit card. I lost my fury to kill around Muncie Indiana - it's that simple & pathetic - I just didn't have the heart for any more killing.

They're some lucky motherfuckers.

✝ ✝ ✝

My sister's first husband hung himself. My mother, sister, & brother found him hanging from the shower rod on a Sunday night. My sister had spent the weekend w/the family & came home to find her husband, swinging from a towel, shit running down his legs. The coroner ruled it an accidental suicide; the insurance money paid for her business degree.

She had her nest egg.

He disappeared.

✝ ✝ ✝

A sick unit, that old father-in-law I had; he molested both of his infant daughters - & his father, their grandfather, joined in their obscenity. I didn't know this till I had been married to her for a year.

I never liked the son of a bitch; he never liked me. I was the one that knocked up his daughter. Sorry, sir - did I beat you to it?

She still called him Dad.

I would've called him dead.

‡ ‡ ‡ ‡

Terrible nightmares... my daughters running thru rice paddies dressed in black pajamas, carrying AKs, a bandoleer across their chests. Feet splashing up water. Their voices are Vietnamese.

I watch them lie in ambush for hours, crouched on the jungle floor, mosquitoes biting their arms & faces. They kill the same American patrol each time, take the weapons & cigarettes & walk off into the swamps.

They eat handfuls of rice under a triple canopy of jungle; all my friends are back there w/them, dipping into that rice, reading letters they stole from the Americans' bodies. One of them is from my mother.

‡ ‡ ‡ ‡

Take a break: there are years full of days that are calm, nothing good or bad happens, just walk right thru 'em like butter. Cash the paycheck, send a check, & get the oil changed. A stack of cans in the cupboard, a loaf of fresh bread & a sinkfull of dirty dishes. Years of not looking past the livingroom couch. Then. One day the old lady in front of you in the grocery store catches a round in the head & the sappers come crawling up the aisles. It begins to feel like home.

‡ ‡ ‡ ‡

I can still remember waking up in different houses, different beds, different women sitting next to my father. My mother spent a few years in the alky hospital when I was 5 or 6; the old man was the guardian of the war.

My brother & I really liked the one red-head he spent the weekends with... bright red lipstick, orange hair, & a Pall Mall laugh. She had a couple daughters we shared a bed with.

The old man smoked cigars in his '56 VW, his hand on the knee of whatever piece of meat was sitting there. My brother puked all over that backseat; I joined him sometimes. We ate most meals at Howard Johnson's.

I didn't recognize my mother when she came to our door. We hadn't seen her for two years; it should have been no surprise to her. We left, like sheep. A new town. A woman named Mother.

The old man should've married that red-head.

‡ ‡ ‡

Coming back from one mission, I ate a facefull of Delta water, felt it squirm in my mouth before I swallowed it, & I still swallowed it. I had sweated my fatigues white under the arms, white down my chest. Hell yes, I drank it.

& got a sweet case of worms, a couple big buggers laid in my gut, eating their cud. Spent a few days at the hospital at Vinh Long where they monitored my bowels, counting the skeletons of worms. I could've kissed each one of them for the vacation.

Everybody on that river had an itchy butt from worms, it came w/the filth. That'd keep you awake at night, scratching.

We gave them such good food.

‡ ‡ ‡

High school, the factory for teenagers. Hit the timeclock, change shifts w/the bell. Bus the workers in, bus them home. Institutional toilet paper & lunches. The rich kids had a clique; the jocks had a clique; the creative kids had a clique; I hung w/ the white trash on the periphery, putting in time on the line. Smoking in the restrooms. Our girlfriends had chipped front teeth & smelled of the projects.

A lot of my friends dropped out, headed for the garages & body shops early. The diploma means nothing when there's a lot of road & no gas in the car.

I played football & it played pussy.

Joey Buehler came home after his graduation, dressed in the rented black robes & put his diploma on the kitchen table. The first kid in that family ever to graduate high school; his father handed him the draft notice that came in the morning mail. He left for the army factory a week later.

‡ ‡ ‡ ‡

The slow dissolve of a man & a woman... you simply stop talking about the future & think about it alone.

Everything I owned had been thrown down the steps, my dresser drawers open & my clothes hanging out. Neighbors watched me from their windows pick it off the steps & load up my truck. The woman inside had the stereo turned up loud but I could hear her laughing on the phone. I pinned a twenty to the door w/a note that read only:

Sorry.

‡ ‡ ‡ ‡

Meghan, I was bygod happy to see your head poke out from your mother's legs the day you were born. You ripped your mother asshole-to-elbow; it took her months to heal from your shoulders. I was ecstatic having you, but kid, frankly I never cared if your mother had died on the table.

I left for Vietnam January 3rd 1975; you were five days old. It was my third time in-country & my last. Security for the remaining Americans.

We did some killing. I spent hours looking at your hospital pictures. You were one cute chipmunk. Still are. I wish you knew me.

‡ ‡ ‡ ‡

Suicide is bullshit, a goddamn vile lie you whisper to yourself when the horror of life weighs more than the graveyard. No one suffers but you. & your dead.

I had less than 1/32 of an inch left on the trigger pull, the barrel pointed right in my mouth; bodies lay on top of the bunkers, 20 VC hung from the wire, a claymore had blown a stack of men all over the field. The ARVN that were left were damn few. We waited on the medevacs for an hour; senselessly, men died all around, VC & ARVN alike, bleeding guts in the sand.

A body moved on the wire & I shot the little bastard.

I really wanted out of there, in an airplane seat, or a bag with my name tag on a toe & I almost made it home. The funeral home already engraved the stone.

✝✝✝✝

She was 23, a registered nurse, worked the steady nights & owned her own home. I was the boyfriend that moved in. I don't know why she let me - she wanted so much more than my memory. She was no looker but a steady attraction.

I stayed a few months till I caught her looking at the walls, waiting on my Viet Cong to slither thru, & I left her without a word.

She had nice curly hair, a quiet laugh, & a scar on her right leg; I don't remember her name. She liked to face the window when she slept.

I didn't sleep much.

✝✝✝✝

Childhood was Vietnam retrofitted.

The old man never saw the turtles, never heard the blade hit their shells; naw, he ran the mower right over them. I spent hours in our backyard finding pieces of small turtles... of course, I shouldn't have let 'em out of the aquarium but... I never said a word to my father.

Same thing w/bunnies & ducks they gave at Easter. They were damn cute in their food-colored fur - blue/purple/pink - & they'd last till the family hated the mess.

I'd find bunnies & ducks strangled in the garbage can. No one ever talked about it, all those temporary animals.

‡ ‡ ‡ ‡

A new guy, a fucking new guy big time od'd on smack. I was cleaning a shotgun outside the barracks when they grabbed me, rather they grabbed my narcan w/my body attached. The kid was new - all of a week in-country - but was learning quick, at least a dozen needle bruises in his arm.

Laying on the floor, next to his rack, the kid's lips were blue, the nailbeds were blue; I tied him off & slid the needle home, loaded w/narcan.

His buddies were playing cards ten feet away, using a makeshift table covered w/a blanket. Not one looked at him. He was new, totally expendable.

His color got better, & he came around.

He did it again the next day & he died on the floor, a middle of-the-night ex-junkie. His name is on The Vietnam Veterans Wall.

‡ ‡ ‡ ‡

I never had a headache till my tour down in the U Minh Forest; sick puke headaches, laying on my back in a mangrove swamp feeling the arteries pound in my head & the puke running down my mouth. I remember being so sick that I couldn't hold my head up, hearing sounds in the bush no animal could make & hoping it was Uncle Charles come to kill the pain.

I was in the hospital for a month before they found an abscess on a lobe of my brain. I still have headaches.

‡ ‡ ‡ ‡

The house smelled of urine; no family member would own up to it but there it is, a carpet stinking of human excrement. I knew my mother was sick.

She'd laugh embarrassingly - oops! - & a dribble flowed.

You had to live there if you wanted to visit.

Friday nights we scrubbed the carpet w/a brush & a bowl of Lysol. A routine, & not thought about. I kept a cigarette burning between my lips just so I wouldn't smell it.

I'll spare her - that's enough.

‡ ‡ ‡ ‡

I came home from Vietnam - for the very last time - thirty days after Saigon fell; my wife had moved back to Minnesota since I had left. I took a taxi a paychecks worth to her apartment. She was asleep - I rang the buzzer hard. She came out in flannel pajamas, her finger to her lips to be quiet. I was.

I walked over to the crib & saw my daughter, a big girl sucking her thumb peacefully. We had coffee in the kitchen; I walked outside to have a cigarette. The baby woke up awhile later & my wife give her the teat. Four months old & already hungrier than two tits - my girl.

She moved the baby in w/her. I had the livingroom. The dog had the run of the house.

All I saw were people leaping for helicopters & the ARVN shooting into crowds. I was pretty comfortable with that.

‡ ‡ ‡ ‡

I have few friends, no one dying in my arms & no one sleeping on my couch. I don't visit myself much either.

I'm comfortable w/a tv, a stereo, & a woman. The Viet Cong are my guests in this apartment, I like their voices in the morning.

I work blue-collar, punch a clock for a living & my legs ache in the evening. A simple man.

But I do keep the door unlocked, both doors unlocked. No one has ever walked thru them.

✝ ✝ ✝ ✝

My ex-wife's sister found God & the Baby Jesus a couple years ago. After laying flat-on-her-back on a hundred backseats of used cars & 6 abortions, she opted for a church pew.

Her daughter is in a foster home, has been for five years. Her son lives at grandma's. Both kids are to different men, neither pay support.

She married a young man, Christian, a few months back & they desperately want children. Immediately.

He bought a mini-van to cart the kids around in.

✝ ✝ ✝ ✝

I waited two hours for the VC tax collector, & he kept to his schedule & I kept to mine. He died. He was carrying a full sack of piastres, levied from the villages he threatened.

I kept that money - bought a woman & some dope.

I've always supported the local economy.

On river patrol we found sampans full of everything: radios imported from Japan, Chinese arms, heroin, people hidden, tons of marijuana going upstream to Saigon, & sometimes

27

medical supplies stolen from our loading docks.

We learned early on to keep what we wanted; a friend of mine had four pounds of 100 pure heroin hidden on his boat. He lived long enough to buy a new Camaro when he got home to Cleveland, then he ate the windshield.

I was never that lucky.

✝ ✝ ✝ ✝

Big black jungle. It'll hold you in its arms & crush the life right out of your heart. A little like closing your eyes tightly & seeing the inside of your brain. Maybe see the worm eat right thru.

A small explosion 200 meters to the right, a flash of 4th of July, the animals turn quiet. Another explosion, this time 225 meters to the right. Relax, the guy firing the tube doesn't know where you are. It'll get noisy in a little while, close your eyes, look at the stars.

& when you finally fall asleep in that pitiful hole you dug, you'll never hear them coming.

I promise.

✝ ✝ ✝ ✝

I was born an alcoholic to an alcoholic, addicted via Mom. I had been told my birth weight was light & that I had spent a few months in the hospital. It wasn't till I was 34 that my sister gave me the truth.

I detoxed in the hospital w/an umbilical attached. No AA for newborns.

✝ ✝ ✝ ✝

Middle of the night laying in bed, staring at the digital alarm clock & hating my life, dreading the future, & not feeling the woman next to me. I go to the bathroom, piss, & then dig in deep under the covers, pull the blanket over my head.

I'm beyond tears, beyond any sorrow; I've looked all the ghosts in the eye & faced my cowardice, my dishonesty. I never look away.

I put my hand on my wife's hip & she pulls it away. You go into hell alone - I know that.

Sweet dreams.

‡ ‡ ‡ ‡

He would scream MOTHERFUCKER! over & over in a firefight, running straight into enemy fire, popping caps methodically as a time card. I saw Hal Wolfe pick a man straight up in the air w/his bayonet then shoot him in the heart.

You had to love him.

It was his third tour in the Nam; it was my first. He had been there since '67, steady, no R&R for that boy. Three years straight in the bush. Wife divorced, kids forgotten, Hal was the goddamn war.

He liked killing personal, a Winchester sniper rifle w/scope or Starlight. He'd lay out in broad daylight under a camouflaged Hessian cloth in an open field & watch the bullet enter the head & the head exit. Next.

Barefoot, he left no boot tracks.

He was still there when I left.

‡ ‡ ‡ ‡

He was insane, totally sociopathic, & I loved him like a father. Pete Casper owned a print shop on the edge of Minneapolis. Every press, every camera, every cutter & folder, all of it, borrowed or stolen from another printer. I worked for him for three years.

His wife had cancer of the throat & answered the phone whispering "printing" - it sounded like a grunt & a cough coupled together. The paper companies wouldn't deliver paper because of his credit. We borrowed trucks to go to their warehouses w/cash.

He moved 8 times in three years; the man paid no rent for three years, none - he'd equipped the presses w/eyebolts so we could forklift them out. I helped him move 8 times. He changed the name of the company each time.

No taxes, no payroll, really no company. We split the cash each week. On a bad week, he'd sell a piece of equipment for a little folding money.

We worked 7 days a week for maybe 3 hours a day, ate all our meals in the shop, & watched a tv when we ran the presses. It had the smell of a heaven.

His wife eventually died, & he moved all the stuff down to Phoenix in the middle of a Saturday night, owing the landlord 4 months of back rent. He opened another shop. & he's sleeping w/a schoolteacher who just happens to have a bit of money.

Dad.

† † † †

I spent the middle 70's reading Reader's Digest condensed books & raising my daughters; I looked forward to my disability check from the VA each month.

Every six months I went for a physical. It was the only time I met other Nam vets; all of us sitting on benches at their disability clinic, smoking cigarettes & waiting for our name to be called. The doctors were bored civil servants. A little clerk gave us travel pay home. It was senseless, but we needed the signature on the government check.

Lots of one-legged, one-armed men in that room. & fury.

The last time I reported for a physical they had security guards in the waiting room.

† † † †

Christmas night, 1969. I'm in the opthamologist's chair - Can Tho City - an army clinic, my head locked into a slit lamp machine, my chin resting on a cup. A young doctor gingerly pulls small pieces of metal out of my left eye.

Our PBR had taken some wicked fire as we rode up a large canal 15 miles north of Can Tho. A rocket had exploded right next to the boat & I went overboard unhurt & unarmed, maybe a bit stunned. The crew was in the water. Two more boats came out the canal, blasting every living thing in the ville w/cannons. A South Vietnamese Navy monitor pulled to twenty feet of the bank & laid in w/its flame thrower. Small arms fire came from the jungle. None of us were killed - a few of them were burned. One of the boats picked us up in the water.

I slept thru the night but couldn't open my eye in the morning. I caught a ride into town w/some Seabees.

The doctor numbed the eye & poured in a fluorescent die. Then he pulled the minute splinters out. I stayed in my rack for two days, puking the pain away. Happy Holidays.

† † † †

Easter Sunday & I was in the woods, firing a .410 shotgun right into the face of a small fox. 14 years old & carrying a shotgun, I was a typical Western Pennsylvania kid.

He was tough, tougher than any deer. He shook his head & snorted, walked on. I shot him again, blowing the legs right out from under him. That gun was tough too.

I walked those woods till dinner & had something to show for myself. I skinned it & threw it away.

††††

One leg shorter than the other & deformed lungs from polio, Ray Augerman was still an asshole. I slept w/his wife on Wednesdays.

She was a beauty, legs right up to her ass, & tits that would take out an eye. Her one kid didn't ruin her vaginal muscles. It was lovely.

He caught me & her in their bedroom, naked as chimps. He had an old Smith & Wesson pistol dangling by his side; I put on my pants & waited on the grave. He never fired - he cried.

I'd have cried too if I had to sleep on that wet spot.

††††

My Aunt Caroline was a recluse, lived in this small red brick house in Connellsville; I don't remember her face but I did help clean the house when she died. One bedroom w/a man's portrait on the wall, a tiny livingroom, & no tv. She spent years - at least fifteen - having groceries & liquor delivered. My mother would try to visit her. We sat in the car w/the locks down, & she talked to my aunt thru a screen door.

I remember the insignificant.

She cleaned her false teeth w/bleach. Her brand of cigarette was Chesterfield's. She had been married once but the family never knew or met him; it lasted less than a heartbeat.

That's all I knew - nothing.

That house was immaculate, as if she never lived there one day. Just spotless.

††††

95% of Vietnam was just hours pounding against the human clock. Boredom, miles of mud & water. Flick a Salem into the water & watch it float downstream.

The horror always came unexpectedly, in a package wrapped so tight you couldn't take your eyes off of it. After the burned & mutilated bodies stopped blinking, your dead best friend would pull up a seat & spend the night w/you, talking out of a contorted face & no mouth at all.

After the first month you pulled so deep into yourself.

I used to check my children in the crib, touch their face & feel their breath on my hand. I was never sure they were alive.

‡ ‡ ‡ ‡

So wonderful, legs hanging out the door of a helicopter flying 300 feet over the heads of farmers, people bent over the rice. A good breeze, the smell of paddy water, & that big ball sun. Recon by air.

It took a committed man or woman to take a potshot at a helicopter; the Viet Cong in the Delta were committed but not stupid. They picked the shots, the ambush, they didn't lose much. They liked to leave us alone, let the boobytraps suck us dry.

Charlie didn't have helicopters.

Ghosts don't fly

‡ ‡ ‡ ‡

Plain of Reeds. Always death in those swamps & canals, always. The VC owned it day & night; they had no weekends off. We mounted missions in there & people died every fucking time. Leeches & water snakes. I saw a guy get sucked so deep into the mud that it took a helicopter to pull him straight up - his boots & pants still in that cesspool.

Charlies loved it in there, miserable terrain & filth. He knew how to dig in. We found a company headquarters in an offshoot of a 6 foot wide canal, actually had to swim into it. They had already left - to god knows where - but they left some food, some rice & fish heads.

We took rubber rafts & skimmer boats down the swamps & canals, using a radar at night to guide us. It was senseless - we were lost more times than not - no matter how many we killed, it changed nothing. It was one hell of a killing ground.

† † † †

A riot in the Pittsburgh Federal Building the day I enlisted & went to boot camp. The guys that had been drafted into the army refused to take the pledge & busted up the waiting rooms, smashing plastic chairs & fake wood tables against the walls.

Federal marshals were called in & they came in breaking heads. Those draftees still didn't pledge undying love to the country; they left on a bus to basic training.

I was on the other side of the hall, the Navy & Marine Corps side. We had all enlisted & were ready to die in our innocence. They nodded their heads in agreement & we took an airplane to Chicago.

The war began.

† † † †

I liked Saigon, been there a couple times visiting the Navy Exchange & had ordered a new Olds 442 thru the GM rep that had an office there. A great deal, pick it up soon as I got home. If I died, my brother could have it.

It was sweet. 19 years old w/a big engine & a cooler in the back. Bronze paint, rally wheels, Hurst shifter. Pop in an eight-track & a two-legged woman. I put 3000 miles on it in a couple weeks. The motor blew outside Baltimore & I left the car on the side of the road. Just walked away.

There was something very wrong w/me.

‡ ‡ ‡ ‡

My hands had been going numb & the headaches were increasing in frequency; I had a skin rash down my legs. & I was snapping apart w/anger.

1979. The VA wasn't owning up to Agent Orange. I had the symptoms & didn't know it. My semi-annual physicals were good, w/elevated liver functions.

A year later we took my youngest daughter to the doctor for a flu she couldn't shake; her blood test came back leukemia. Good remission rate w/leukemia, they told me. They didn't say little kids died. She started chemotherapy, just out of diapers. I can barely write this, thinking of her in a hospital bed, bald & crying; I was insane for grief long before she died.

‡ ‡ ‡ ‡

He wasn't paying any attention & my IV was backing blood up the tubing; I was on the medevac sandbags adding my fluids to the slime.

Two buddies helped me in there minutes before, my IV bag was thrown to the floor. I was just a leg wound, a no big deal, no ticket home. The guy right next to me - an army trooper from a unit that got waxed - was absently tugging at a piece of his intestine, trying to stick it back in the hole. I never saw a grayer face. The corpsman slapped a large dressing on his stomach & hit him w/ Morphine.

I pulled the IV out of my own arm & got a taste of that morphine. They could've sawed my fucking legs right off.

They were friendly, Jack & Faye Cummings. Lived right across the street from us in Norfolk & they helped furnish our house w/used junk when we moved in, barely married a year.

He was a Navy lifer right at the end of his twenty. Jack saw the coast of Vietnam from an aircraft carrier. He & his wife liked Uncle Sammy well enough to cash his checks for the rest of their lives.

Our wives were instant sisters. We got along just fine - I gave him gas money every week & we drove to the base in his big black Buick... till the day my wife showed off our bedroom to Faye & she noticed the trail of bloodstains leading to the bathroom.

I drove 1972 myself.

† † † †

My mother had been home only two weeks before I found the first hidden bottle. I dumped it out & sat Mr. Gilbey's on her night stand.

I had saved all the bloody rags she had vomited in, a stack of white wash cloths & towels turned permanently pink from her esophageal hemorrhage.

She waved me off.

I came back months later & every cupboard & drawer had a bottle stuck in it. The old lady was always a mover.

† † † †

I rushed her into the mall, so damn cold outside that my eyelashes formed icicles - really. The windchill was 45 below nothing but my daughter wanted a Baskins-Robbins ice-cream. I had wrapped her up tight, barely a face sticking out. I covered her w/a blanket. She was right at the end of her leukemia what she wanted, I made sure she had.

The little kid ate the ice cream cone, then another one. Gulped 'em down. Her grey eyes were big but the circles under them were huge.

She sat in my lap as I had a coffee. I tickled her very very lightly; her ribs were sticking right thru her skin... so emaciated I could see the blue veins in her face.

But it was a good moment, one of the last.

‡ ‡ ‡ ‡

Delayed Stress Syndrome.

He was a new kid, a helper on the press next to mine, barely nineteen w/a mouthful of snuff. He was going to spend the day dipping ink out of a press, changing plates, & loading paper - sweating bad for the minimum.

& he dropped a carton of paper to the floor, it must've weighed a good 150 & exploded. I went to the floor, looking for the mortar flash. Ready, real ready for a firefight. My heart pounding my ribs, goddamn adrenaline closing my throat & my vision.

I remembered where I was & it embarrassed me so much I walked over & squeezed his neck hard, warning him.

Delayed Stress Syndrome.

‡ ‡ ‡ ‡

No way out but the grave. I'm going to ride this whore Vietnam straight down the ovarian death; I don't think about the war, it thinks about me, loves me, holds my face in its charred arms & grins.

Everybody I knew is dead, fucking gone, alive only in my mind; I have this terrible responsibility to keep them walking, fill their veins w/blood & move their lips. I got to count on these words.

This is crazy. I'm still reliving firefights that existed for only minutes - mygod, I've thought about them & seen them behind my eyes for hundreds of hours. Some of the horror can not be mouthed. There are no words to describe a scream.

Maybe I would've fucking blown it w/o Vietnam.

Most probably.

But I don't know why every relationship I've ever had w/a woman has turned to shit soup. The only constant is me. I don't have the stomach to look at all the lives I've mangled.

I have two .44 mags under my couch & one more in the car. They ease the pain. One day they'll take all the pain & drive it down to the butcher shop.

All day I fought suicide & I won. I've nailed my right hand to this chair, stuck my knife right thru it to the wood. I type w/the other.

Because if I'm not bleeding, it ain't worth the reading.

I know nothing else

GHOST POEMS

the dark & bloody ground
I too wanted more from the years than searing nightmares
broken marriages & a body that's frayed in the seams

this morning I woke up in an ez chair
a cigarette long burned into my fingers

I put the gun under the sofa
& splashed handfuls of cold water in my face

my wife sleeps in another room with a clock radio
her nightgown torn from a night many years ago

I walk past her room wanting badly to quietly open
the door & slip under the covers with a woman I once knew

but I've sentenced myself to another year in Vietnam
its fingers gripped tightly around my neck in dreams

I sit too many nights traveling in my chair
smelling the gut wounds of strangers who scream my name

the last man out of Saigon

you have ghosts, you have everything
I knew that Vietnam would play in my eyes till the day I drop
the growl of the war would always be my nights

I thought I would be dead before the body gave out
standing outside Pittsburgh's VA hospital with a bandage

on my throat I rubbed the small stitches till blood
spotted the small white compress

the man who'd slashed it died years ago
I've spent whole days seeing his face explode

& his body falling backward into the sandbags of a bunker
the knife still in his hand

he walked away dead
the winner

the dead walk the earth
walking thru minefields of my desire
my boots slosh & leak blood

I've become my own ghost

no shadows where I run the nights
thru the taste of the blade in my throat
& the silence of the dead

I slip my fingers thru a mirror
& pull out the beating heart
of a man I once knew so well

that I killed him

pictures of a dream
this last one almost finished me
my dead mother leaned over my bed to give me a kiss

her face badly wrinkled & flushed with vodka
giggling she pulled my dead daughter off her breast

& dropped her on my stomach
where her vomit lingered for hours

1/5/91
I went to bed this morning dressed in my best clothes
a close shave & clean underwear

I lay there till four in the afternoon
my finger still on the triggerguard of a .38

I put one round thru the wall
& another into the mirror

killing that sick bastard
who never dies

the peace of all
I killed
for a plane ticket home

to live in an alcoholic mother's house
& watch her die slowly for years

in a heap
we crumbled together

doppelganger
I read in the paper that another Vietnam veteran
in this 2 block town took a shotgun blast to his head

he was survived by a wife & two teenage children
services for immediate family only

I checked the address twice
it wasn't mine

I walk with zombies
formaldehyde runs thru my veins
I let my soul die meaninglessly in Vietnam

& frankly, I don't want it back
my marriages & children live along the skin

I keep a gun hidden under the seat in my car
another under my pillow

I gave the bottle up for straight shots of horror
pulling the hammer back on a .38 & feeling the metal

cold on my throat till the sweat runs down my ribs
& the devil himself bows a bit

alive, in the flames
I make no apologies for Vietnam
the dead have by now rotted thru their caskets

settling only into the haunted minds of all of us
who see the war fresh every day

I've paid for the bloodstains on my hands with my life
the only forgiveness is the truth
of a headstone

the long drone of years
there is no end to the burning bodies stacked in my mind
when one day in Vietnam is over, another lights a candle

its silhouette plays the length of my bedroom wall
small splotches of blood dot the curtains & rug

I sit up in bed watching the muzzle flashes & hear
the screams of wounded men dragging themselves over the wire

some nights I see my own daughters dressed in black pajamas
tourniquets on their arms & legs as they walk the paddies
with the mutilated ghosts of dead Viet Cong I killed years ago

it's only true
I'd drop right now
if there was no shame
to my death rattle

a permanent tourist
I imploded inside a small efficiency apartment
my blood ran on the landlord's couch & bed

the windows were held together with duct tape
cockroaches ran out of my stove's burners

I spent two years there thinking about my daughter's death
I'm sure my heart stopped but the meter kept running

all thru those Minneapolis winters
I stopped dreaming about Vietnam

there was one greater hell

pig pen
I paid for the killing alone in a small room
every man & woman I shot in Vietnam lay down beside me

& made me feel their wounds
my hands wrung miles out of intestines

I slept with their heads wrapped around me
under the blankets I felt their hands

the room smelled of carrion & pools of blood
I've never felt more alive

ghost poem
it's the time of night when the beards of the dead grow
I close my eyes not to see them these ghosts of the Vietnam dead

They've stolen my skin to become human
- my blood pounds their eyes wide

I'll walk the night thru this apartment
breathing hard under the weight of bodies

this is all such bullshit
I ended my life years ago

ghost poem
they cuddle close to my wife those amputees
& sucking chest wounds from the Nam

grunts lay next to her as she sleeps
they curl her hair in their muddy fingers

I can smell them when I open the door
& follow blood trails to the bed

I hate the smile on her face

ghost poem
they flit & flutter like dead hummingbirds
the ghosts of the Viet Cong sip my blood

their faces uplifted toward me ripping tendons to get my jugular
I let them have a taste

sometimes a whole patrol jumps me on the couch
smothering me with red-eyed hate as they stick fingers into bodies

pulling out bullets that I once fired or fragments of a grenade
they've given me parts of my own body back in the form of rice

ghost poem
I check myself: 2 arms/2 legs
no blood on the pillow

one more night alive & dead
an old Vietnamese ghost whistles from the couch

he hands me fingers of his children
I give him the heads of mine

ghost poem
I fight the knife
21 years fighting

Vietnam has been
routine suicide

my daughters will never
understand I saved them

by my absence

ghost poem
I slip in my blood
the shrapnel in my hands

burns the bones 2 million Vietnamese
walk the skies dead as light

We rocked the cradle
magnificently

ghost poem
I die
furiously

a hundred thousand
hours of Vietnam

have slithered
in my dreams

my fists
still go thru walls

& out the other side

my wife is gone
the kids too

the job
is always burning down

I sleep
in the arms

of war

ghost poem
I'm reduced by memories
pathetic middle-aged man

knows himself by Vietnam
too comfortable with horror & mutilation

a gunshot in the dark
my finger is already on the trigger guard

I look right down the barrel
with my mouth I'm too angry

for suicide tonight
maybe
not

ghost poem
I keep waiting on a bullet my whole life I've waited
I watched a teenager in Vietnam fire a round in my body

another slit my throat
I'm more comfortable with the handles of a coffin

than a credit card
my door is <u>always unlocked</u> here in

Youngwood
PA

my bullet is anonymous

ghost poem
I dream black Vietnam horror
I've ruined mattresses throwing a bad night

out in the street I'm shaking
this morning wanting blood

a bullet wound into the past

I've often seen my own death
grey lips blood-livid legs

eyes like a doll
I can feel the undertaker

powder my face with ground bone

I wish my dead mother was here
when I come home

ghost poem
I die to live
my head has fallen onto this keyboard

no more words about Vietnam
I stink daily from its plague

my dreams rob graves
the jewelry of the dead hang from my neck

I wash myself off the mirror
shining like a bullet

ghost poem
I just sit here for hours
dead numb staring at the walls

I think of nothing
not even death

I left more
than my fingers

in
Vietnam

ghost poem
light casualties tonight one man down
lightly dying

ghost poem
an hour ago I had my hands on my wife
huddled under a comforter I lost my death for a moment

she sank her hands right through me
& blooded the sky with my bones

ghost poem
I swish a little blood around my mouth
spit & rinse with peroxide

the nightmares of war hold so little blood
my bedsheets hold the dying white

a stainless steel bucket is filled with mangled
arms & legs a rib hangs over the side

the only screams are in my head

ghost poem
I have everything: cans of soup & a gun

the door is always open
& a candle lit for the dead

I'll be in the back room pounding the demons

into a keyboard
I'd offer a chair

maybe peel some Vietnam off my bedroom wall
I'll give you my head you give me a life

ghost poem
The end of my little finger is still rotting in Vietnam
buried in the silt of a paddy feeding rice & fish
it took such little talent to be shot
I fed my own
grave

ghost poem
I'm still losing parts of me in Vietnam
my brain dangles behind a dying body

I turn my head
& the bodies fall

I don't know why these severe memories
of war keep me alone & bloody in my boots

there is so much
I don't talk about

it kills me

ghost poem
twice this week I almost kissed
the face of a train

ghost poem
so easy to die
so hard to live

I put out the light shut off the clock
stretch my legs against my wife

stare at the shadows in the dark
turn the machine on that stops my throat

from collapsing in sleep & take in a deep breath
Vietnam is an eyeblink away

I'm not looking

ghost poem
I didn't die young

furious
I'm 40

I've been shot

stabbed
& left

I would've sold the sky
for a soul
my wife is in another room
waiting on a man without my face
without my history

ghost poem
I've laid in bed for hours propped
up on pillows staring at the rafters
wondering if they would hold my weight

they will
I won't

I don't know why a war has made me feel
so bad so long

everyday
I feel

the noose tighten

ghost poem
I've scarred my knuckles broken every finger
cracked the windows on most of the cars

I've owned with my fists
I'm so scared of losing myself

in the fury of Vietnam
I've kept the anger
lost a life

ghost poem
I never did call the VA back
this morning my tolerance

for misery is enormous
I understand wheelchairs

artificial limbs old men dressed
in camouflaged fatigues

howling at the moon
for our own skin

nobody laughs at our tears
anymore

the sunrises are still
beautiful in Vietnam

ghost poem
it's so pointless to live in the cradle of Vietnam
every Vietnam veteran I know is still walking on the Moon

with his own copyrighted scream of horror
I don't know any way out

I'm so damn exhausted sucking the sugar tit of war
everything reminds me of Vietnam

so little left for my wife
but more words

ghost poem
I am a mourner left at the grave
my eyes bleed a trickle runs

down my cheek every day
another day

the ghosts of the Viet Cong
nod their heads gnashing teeth

they like my pain
me too

ghost poem
the room hums
I sleep in white noise

a brilliant fire
of hell

A big blue Vietnam sky
I lay on my back

watch the dead
float by

ghost poem
I don't feel lousy enough to die today
five hours dreams last night

a warm shower without blood
ate cold spaghetti for breakfast

two pots of coffee a trip to the post office
my wife is still in bed I can hear her shifting

I think about my daughters then change the subject
turn the tv on stare out the window

an old face stares back
dead as hell

ghost poem
nothing to lose
nothing to win

I don't know when the bullshit ends
& the dreams begin the small spots of blood

on the floor are real fresh red human paint
I woke up from another nightmare screaming into an oxygen mask

two hours ago an empty bed
I need something more than Vietnam & myself

something less real
goddamn every one

ghost poem
I don't have any excuses
without Vietnam I felt like a victim

everything around me
bled thru the nose

I started life in 1985 blaming
only myself for myself

the war didn't kill my marriage
lose my daughters my job

I did

sometimes I can't hear
for the screams

ghost poem
I sweat ghosts in this room
the dead bead on my forehead

run down my sides pool in my crotch
they like my guns & old pictures

I have from Vietnam some recognize themselves
they clap their hands smear mud on their faces

olive-drab dead faces
I offer my cheek

they accept

ghost poem
I don't think the country is ever going to forgive us
for throwing up our hands & dying in Vietnam
our dead lay in small picture frames above a family's tv dusted
occasionally - forever 19 years old in boot camp uniforms
the ones that came home in pieces & chunks are there too quietly
the suicides take a frame on a bedroom dresser
the living spin in graves covered by the dirt of fear
their country sticks a miniature flag on their lapel
they cry in empty apartments too full of themselves
trusting no one but rooms of empty air & pale green walls
I remember a time when we had friends that would die for us

ghost poem
a dead god's dead child
I don't feel guilt for the scorched bodies

left in Vietnam I participated
they participated death fits all boxes

I feel terrible alive & well
my heart walks on its own feet

& it feels
shame alone

ghost poem
undefeated
& lost

I hang my mouth

on a moon
& a gun

the captain lied: the boat is leaking
all day I've thought about a corpse I found
on the bank of the My Tho river without a head/arm/2 legs
a body without steam

on my shoulder
Death comes

to cry

ghost poem
I remember feeling my own exposed bones
in a firefight that lasted five deaths
flies found us immediately

traitors
& rats

repeating
Vietnam

own this world
& our blood has dripped
from the cradle
mixed with slow dirty
tears
a snout of ooze

silence

ghost poem
on my bed the moon sweats
in the house of the hanged man
we don't talk the noose
I write for all those dead mouths

every day is
Father's Day

& all the men are dead
the night so black I taste it between my teeth
the light is always burned out in my lamp
curtains closed & a gun loaded

I sit in a 10' x 15' room
bigger than all of Vietnam
& much more deadly

ghost poem
a piece of my nightmare
was torn out
& hung on The Vietnam
Veterans Memorial Wall
I pay
the rent hourly
the jungle wild on

my shoulder & outside
there's a tree
where birds
come to die

a pure ghost poem
I don't want to hear your version of Vietnam
until you have the courage to hold your dying mother's head

as she fills your lap with bloody vomit
& dies in your arms

think of that moment for twenty odd years
remember what you said or more importantly, what you didn't do

dream of your cowardice your absolute fear
& smell the room she held you
inhale the blood and hair
walk in her bones till your wife finds you
crying in a back room or a garage

I'll be there with you
bawling like a newborn

ghost poem for Blacky Hix
it took too many years & 3 quarts of a stranger's blood to finally
arrive in this dark backroom

I tried killing myself w/sadness
bound around a Seconal addiction & a marriage
littered by the hounds of hell.
I lived for the lack of anything else to do

fearing a death I wouldn't attend
all excuses become lies in a small room
facing eyes in the dark you betrayed
till only Vietnam was left & it too felt soft as a dream

on the day I was born
God was sick

it's taken me 40 years not to give a damn

a short poem about a Vietnam veteran in Youngwood PA
The first time
I was shot

I was ashamed of my mortality;
the second time, I died.
Just ask my wife.

a ghost poem
I look in the mirror & it isn't a young man looking back;
one more middle-aged man with scars & saggy eyelids

too many furnished rooms
too many used b&w tv sets w/aluminum foil antennas
too many checks to an ex-wife too many children
too many nights alone too many nights w/the wrong women

too many years sticking my tongue down the throat of Death
too many years bleeding guts on the grave of Vietnam

too many lives for one man too many deaths for anyone
I look in the mirror
no one looks back

a 1978 ghost poem
I remember picking up the children the next day
their suitcases packed & leaning next to a sink of dirty dishes

their father was dead their mother too

one grandmother sat w/the kids rocking the baby in her lap
 a two year old girl twirled the barrettes in her hair

the dog was already in my car
the bodies were already at the funeral home
we had bled together in Vietnam
now he bled w/his wife alone in a cold room

I never saw the shotgun but I saw the walls
we stopped for candybars & cokes on the way home

a ghost, ghost poem
I wake up so confused some nights that I stare at the wall
watching for a man to walk right thru

I could've sworn there were leeches on my arms
a water snake curled around my leg

a small gunshot hole appears in my chest
& it pins me to the bed bloody foam hisses out my side

in the dark I can't even whisper my own name
take the pain, Bill Shields, take the pain
never cry out never give away your position
take the pain quietly
it's 3:00 a.m. 9/7/91 in Youngwood PA
I'm in my crib banging at the rails w/my tears
dying in my own arms with no grace at all

a ghost poem
she walked out two hours ago just put on her coat
& found her car keys
calmly opened the kitchen door & began a different life

so simple
& probably right

I was six hours out of Vietnam still shaking a bit on the couch
watching tv w/a knife in one hand sipping coffee w/the other
I've never hit a woman
but I would've killed her if she had spoken a word

that's a lie...
I asked her to slit my throat

my hands were shaking too much to do a really good suicide
& she refused
the end

ghost poem
I'll never write about flowers when all I hear are screams
& the ticks of blood on the floor
voices of the dead announced my marriage vows & their hands
pulled my children's heads out of their mother

at birth they sat w/me nights when the pain of being alive
overwhelmed my fear of death
those 2 million Vietnamese

aren't greedy for my blood they're willing to wait
for my heart to explode

ghost poem
an empty bed a dirty kitchen
I slept in my clothes again last night
dead on the couch w/an old magazine
waking up to blood pounding in my throat
seeing God's head stuck on a bamboo pole

a large pig roots at the dirt in front of it
I scratch myself awake yawning at the familiar

one more tooth shattered
23 to go

ghost poem, 10/3/91
my shame eats flesh
my own flesh
I killed my daughter w/Agent Orange

myself w/grief

21 years since Vietnam 8 years since her death
I've forgotten nothing I've forgiven nothing

a little older now a lot more fragile
the streets are always deserted to men like me
asleep in a single bed

Mom, don't worry I won't be there for Christmas dinner
promise

ghost poem
I've died too soon
my blood scarcely mattered

I was married once had children
divorced remarried

& before all that I went to Vietnam
& after all that I went to Vietnam

I saw the earth splashed in blood
souls stabbed out of living bodies

children dead in their mother's stomachs
human bodies blended with high speed steel

I only believed in myself

& today
I forgot

ghost poem
I just want one day without a memory of Vietnam
24 hours blind/deaf/dumb

no smells of napalm a nude landscape painted w/Agent Orange
nothing to remind me of dead friends

I want a day without seeing
my daughter's face in a hospital bed

dying of cancer bald & emaciated
feeling her hand fall away when she died

no more
Hell

God,
I've had enough

ghost poem
I've been killed so many times my ghost is a dead fly in a corner
of the room
I sleep w/napalm burning above the bed like a goddamn brilliant
sunrise in Vietnam

the floor rattles old Chinese bayonets & U.S. canteens my walls
are from an operating room theater outside Saigon

I've thrashed this bed till water sprang from it –
the wails of the killed-in-action lick the bedpost

this is a good place to die
a good time

ghost poem
I coated the bed in blood one more night
my hair matted to the pillow
I tore it away

ripped myself from the bed to the shower
where the water ran a red massacre to the drain

my right eye burst a vessel & the rest went out my nose
I can't even remember the nightmare except

I'm sure it was about Vietnam

it always is
I never dream of love but I do sleep w/women
unless they scream in their sleep

more than me
& then

I sleep better

ghost poem
what kind of woman would want to sleep with a Vietnam veteran
she'd cry for the both of 'em for a few years & leave rightfully

most mornings she would've faced the leftovers of a bad night the
sheet changed but the bruises burn for days
maybe not in every house but always my house

ghost poem
I kicked it all square in the teeth
even without Vietnam I would've kissed my ass goodbye
the jails & marriage & children I crushed in my hands
bloody from contagious neglect they no longer squirm
I set myself up for failure
the first time I crapped my pants in the cradle
& later, in absolute fear, in a Vietnam jungle
years in these small efficiency apartments with my stench
regretting everything & living nothing blind in dead time
I can't be comforted with words or waving hands
there won't be a Second Coming in this room
but if you want,
I can tell you about the time
I stayed awake all night listening to a dead man's body
he was an okay guy

ghost poem
it wasn't till yesterday I knew in my veins
that the pain the suffering I have from Vietnam is never going to end

no woman holding me in the night or in the shower
no small child whispering <u>Daddy</u> from a dark crib

I'm going alone with this one
3 hours sleep last night sitting in the livingroom

watching cable till my eyes fell to the stars
waking up unsure what state or country I was in

I chewed the inside of my mouth
felt my eyes with my hands
& turned the coffeemaker on
the heads of the dead children cracked

I said good morning to my wife

ghost poem
I don't trust anybody not even you
the years have been too hard too many scars, too many miles

we didn't know each other's name in the Nam
I don't want to know it now

my suffering is no different than yours
I want to die every day

misery isn't brotherhood
I got a gun

you got a gun
I wish we cared enough to pull the trigger

ghost poem
I wish I had a horse to kill
something big bloody & breathing

a sad night tonight big time regrets
the phone has rung twice w/ex-wives wanting their check

tomorrow's Thanksgiving & I feel like a horse
yeah a baked fucking horse

I'll send the ex-wives their checks w/a plate of horsemeat
for the children

ghost poem, for my son
I've written w/my back against the gun
the words pounding my fingers to machines
more than a few nights I've laid a gun on the keyboard
waited on the poem w/intent

no one has ever seen the tears that have run down my face
when the words eat my heart & chew holes in my throat

I've given up on love
& settled for horror

one more piece of bond
I can stamp my name & address on a short poem below it
I ain't asking for much

a little air/a little room
more ammunition

ghost poem
no one could have saved me
I can't blame a wife or my kids

I've never turned around
& I don't look at mirrors

Christ was never a sleeping pill
I've believed in nothing

4 years since I last went to jail
16 since drug addiction

I've killed more cars than men

I have tried to write about anything but Vietnam for the last year & a half
continually failing

even now
I wanted to tell you what a fuckup I've been

& it just feels like more of that goddamn war

ghost poem
I fought so hard to stay alive for two tours of Vietnam
I won't put the gun in my mouth now but I'll think it

maybe let a little gun oil soak into my lips
chip a front tooth on the barrel
I did <u>anything</u> to come home from that war & I did it twice
every day was going to be Christmas
pure gravy, a full plate of mashed potatoes
I promised myself a damn good life if I lived
no regrets
so why do I sit here night-after-night w/a loaded pistol in my lap
the answer is a lie

ghost poem
I only wanted one woman to hold my head when the blood of
Vietnam ran down my face
one person to listen to the bones crack in my nights
w/o running to her car & then her family's livingroom

with tales of my personal horror
I recorded my suicide twenty-one years ago
there is nothing to fear but suffocating sadness

& a pair of wild eyes

ghost poem
6'4"
240 lbs.

Vietnam vet
ex-husband

father
& ghost

I've known suffering
like the odor of a burger
cooking in its fat my own fat
all I have left is my skin
& a light wallet
I don't hope for anything
the plaster falls
walls crumble
I take 2 more antacids
a sip of coffee
there is nothing
else

A LIME GREEN HELL

Brain tumor. Epilepsy. Spinal cord trauma.
His wife took the kids & the car a month back. He was stuck in the top floor of a broken house with their furniture, the kids' toys under his feet, & the sour smell of milk, probably from a bottle hidden under the baby's crib.

The aquarium was dead; even the sludge sucker floated belly-up. He didn't change the water. He was never going to change that water. The refrigerator beneath it dripped on the floor.

Chicago, Winter of '76.
He was hitchhiking to work, hitchhiking home. Walking for groceries. 40 dollars left for two weeks of food, the rest went to his wife in St. Paul.

& he began passing out, fainting with his eyes closed.

The phone didn't ring. No one knocked on the door. He was alone on the horse.

& he still is

alive.

+ + +

The Drone of a Compressor
You could see weeping willow trees from the nicotine stained window; they liked the humidity, the oppressive heat of hell. It was the Navy barracks, set right off a black grinder of a parking lot, a dull green home of dull.

Sit in a room, listen to the next guy snore. The front gate was five miles away, & there was nothing outside of it but jewelry stores & bad restaurants. Cheap motels & whores. Used car lots. Bars.

On paydays the bathrooms were coated in puke from teenagers licking the rim of Southern Comfort.

I propped my head up on the pillow for hours with the lights out, the radio on; AM station singing.

The needle slid in sweet.

♦ ♦ ♦

pulling steel
Every year since his departure from Vietnam, he's lost a finger, or a toe, or a muscle or tendon, or teeth. One year he lost a wife. Another, a child.

There was a time - a twentieth anniversary of sorts - that he lost himself. Like a badly rotted tooth, dropped & left in some forgotten drawer.

I see him occasionally in the bathroom mirror, his eyes still glaring with blood.

I don't look at him twice.

♦ ♦ ♦

19 inches of a green screen tv
Dingy white wall hadn't been painted in a dog's age. Headlights & people's faces bounced off the wood work in nightmare lime - the tv was on. Kids stared right into the tube, heads held by miniature hands.

It was a black & white set, with a piece of green plastic glued to the tube. The old man liked it like that. It stayed like that. Period.

Kennedy was killed on that tv.

Vietnam was started on it.

It was a damned television.

✦ ✦ ✦

just a sad little story
God didn't save him.

Love wouldn't.

Routine kept him sane. He woke up the same time every morning, made coffee before he showered, packed his lunch for work & left. He knew his job like an old wallet. & he left work the same time every day.

He wasn't happy yet he wasn't entirely miserable. As if the joy & the horror of life occurred everywhere but between his sheets, his skin. He sat for hours listening to his own silence, wanting more than himself, & not getting it.

He forgot his name on the weekends.

✦ ✦ ✦

not an ounce of hope
He had the desire to leave that house forever but not the courage. She looked at him as if he was a child, fumbling in his pockets for an answer or a cookie. The evenings were quiet; they were both tired from work & anxious for comfortable silence.

& it went on for years, insipidly.

She died first, from lung cancer. He had that whole house alone. It was with a perverse joy that he kept the toilet seat up

& a turd floating in the water.

✦ ✦ ✦

Veteran
A dead man. He continually felt his arms & legs, squeezed them real hard, feeling the pulse in his wrist, the thump of an artery in his thigh. It became a habit, like driving his car & counting his breaths per minute.

He spoke to the anonymous faces we all talk to.

& he felt nothing.

No visions, no apparitions, no wraiths, no nothing. Just a supreme empty grave inside his body, ready for his mind.

Without pain

he ate dirt.

+ + +

This Could Be Me
A hard wistfulness. More memories than furniture.

He was locked in the breech of the past - locked, loaded, & living. He allowed himself a bed & a change of clothes. An old boombox sat on the floor next to the mattress, tapes scattered across the bare floor.

A year's worth of newspapers in the kitchen. Library books stacked to a man's chest. A manual typewriter sat on the landlord's kitchen table.

There was blood on the wall turned to black; he no longer saw it.

& on a decent summer night he'd be on that wobbly front porch with a bottle of Gordon's & a radio turned to the ballgame

screaming at the Vietnamese.

+ + +

A Bad Day in December 1974
The boat had already sunk.

I sat outside on the driveway staring at the stars - wishing bychrist a meteor would melt me right into the ground. Not a trace of this body left. A mind left in slush.

71

My daughter was born the next day.

She changed nothing.

Nothing at all.

＊ ＊ ＊

You Want To Know What It's Like?
I saw the first shot coming

right at my face. A muzzle flash a millisecond before from the side
of the trail. The bullet beginning to tumble, spinning a hole
through the air; it knew the placement of my eyes, & the soft spot
between them.

& when it missed, hitting the stump of a tree. I didn't thank God.

I killed that little motherfucker.

＊ ＊ ＊

Boom Boom.
Reasons. Rooms full of reasons.
Disgusted, he threw the pillow against the wall.
Everybody got their reasons, he thought.
She had her reasons for leaving.
He had his for dying.
The real story was the lie. The lies.

His life began & ended in Vietnam, & he was sick of it. But there
had been no way she could've understood that he had watched a
friend die in 13 seconds & had done nothing but hate himself

for the rest of his life.

Just reasons. Rooms full of reasons.

. . .

Dreaming Of Saigon

Every day spent in that hole of a room was a day closer to the
coroner's slab; I paced that small floor over & over, stepping only
in my last footprint. Furious, coldly furious.

I stuck a gun in every corner, & one next to the bed.

thinking:

when I stop brushing my teeth, my brains are going to be on the
wall.

Yes indeed.

. . .

Rattlesnakes on Fire

A day measured in cigarettes; he threw the empty pack in the
garbage as he went to bed. He woke habitually at 2:00 a.m. & peed.
Lit a cigarette on the can. An old song - the title he could never
remember - ran through his head every night in the bathroom.

He would stare out the window at the headlights on the street...
then go back to bed. Think of the woman he should've married, the
kids that might've looked like him, a job he wouldn't hate so much

& sigh loud enough to wake the cat.

If there had been someone to blame, he would've thrown a life right
on their shoulder.

But he'll turn, head back to bed

knowing nothing is waiting right there.

◆ ◆ ◆
Her Lips, His Eyes, & All That Hair
By the time he made it home from work, she was throwing his last pair of socks into the alley. His stereo & books were parked in his parking space; there was a trail of underwear & clothes to the garbage cans.

He pulled the car in, the crunch of books under the tires, & slowly, very slowly, his head fell against the steering wheel.

Later, he opened the car door & fell out

of heaven.

◆ ◆ ◆
The Stench of Danger & Pain
The more he tried to make that room a home

the more that room became a room

The right pictures of children & old parents hung from the wall; the dishes were laid out neatly in a plastic rack. His socks were folded into themselves, stuck in pairs into an immaculate drawer.

He dusted once a week, like his & her mother. The bathroom sink shined, staring back at him. His toothbrush was stuck on the rack with three empty holes next to it.

His smell was everywhere.

That desperate sweat.

◆ ◆ ◆
My Name is Bill Shields
It was insane

& he knew it.

A dirty plastic bag dropped over his head & tied at the throat by his one necktie. It was the quietest place in the world. He closed his eyes & all the bills were paid & a woman was waiting for his arms.

The moment before he died

had been worth his whole life.

♦ ♦ ♦

A Lime Green Hell - A Prose Haiku
The last thing I said to my mother before she died was a lie. I forgave her.
...tonight I'm thinking a lot about my death, & my own kids. They'll lie to me too.

& watch the blood collect in my lower legs.

♦ ♦ ♦

Mutilation
Lobotomized by Vietnam...

She should've thrown his head & body out of the house years before. He owed her money; he owed his ex-wife money; he owed himself money.

The jobs never quite worked out.

He never slept in their bed; actually, no one ever saw him sleep. He walked the alley outside their apartment late at night, talking to himself in a voice softer than a whisper, fingering the tiny military can opener he carried with his keys.

& when he drank, that can opener walked the walls.

She eventually pitched him & all that unspoken sadness.

He evaporated back to America.

75

* * *

Sweethearts of the rodeo
Over a plate of cold pasta,

she began to hate his cute eyes, the raw pull of his mouth, that crooked index finger on his right hand, his chipped canine tooth; his mannerisms tasted like acid to her eyes.

They had been married for fifteen years - living in a slaughter house of silence.

It felt like home when the cattle screamed for the axe.

* * *

A bright red boat coming up the river
"That's my evening," his wife said, placing a warm bottle of bourbon on the coffee table.

"Here's mine," he replied

& his head hit the concrete.

* * *

The hellhounds sat up & begged
The poison was insidious. He waited year after year for it to dissolve & cannibalize his organs - to wake up one morning coughing up blood from a lung, or pee it from a kidney tumor.

Everything had been temporary, a thousand jobs & a few beaten wallets. Women sensed his dissipation & he slept with his own body.

Another can of beer. Another filter cigarette.

Pennsylvania was so banal

with Agent Orange.

∗ ∗ ∗

The courage of an idiot
He had spent too much time

not to kill her. For weeks, the only desire in his head had been her death. Her hot blood was flowing through his fingers, her hair was already in the garbage can - with her head.

No more, he said to himself, no fucking more. I've hated her long enough.

& so

she killed him.

∗ ∗ ∗

1979
Ten years of silence. Not even his best friend knew he was a Nam vet. He spent eighteen hours a day sweeping bodies under the rug.

His room became a temple to the past; Vietnam pictures on the wall, a Purple Heart hung on a string from the ceiling, fatigues tacked to a window, & a loaded .45 on the dresser. No one was ever invited into that room - it belonged to the dead.

& when he died in a one car accident

all the minister could say at the funeral was what a good high school football player he had been.

Amen.

∗ ∗ ∗

it's only love
What he touched

his children killed. A marriage, a scruffy mutt that hid beneath the covers, his favorite books, & the backseat of a car. All in ruins or dead.

He set their room on fire.

The ghosts danced in his head.

Nothing died.

✦ ✦ ✦
Pissing in the kitchen sink
If I had had a flamethrower... My mother went to AA; every Wednesday she quit drinking.
By Friday, there were always two paperbags full of empty vodka bottles in the garbage can, along with bits of her hair & skin.

Her red eyes stared out from under the lid

✦ ✦ ✦
The Rapture.
He began disappearing

slowly, a bone at a time. It became a habit, lightly tapping his right arm, then his left leg, making sure they were still hanging from his body; he'd look down at his feet, then touch his nose... scratch his nose.

His life had gone to hell slowly & comfortably.

The furniture vanished over the years, with a wife & kids & office.

Just a sleeping bag left in the corner of an unfurnished apartment & a stack of tv dinner trays piled in the sink. A slight whiff of urine.

He weights his pants down with quarters

dimes & nickels.

+ + +

A baby taken from the toilet
Forget the <u>why</u>

atrocity follows atrocity.

He mutilated the bodies, limbs & faces thrown & interchanged; a
two year old child stuck to the half-ripped bosom of a wrinkled old,
old woman, burned to a black crisp. His finger dug the eyes out of
a dead teenager. His feet went right through the ribs of a dead NVA.

He pissed into the graves that rocked hundreds of lime-coated
bodies.

& he lived through the war

but his coffin will be carried by thousands.

+ + +

Last night, when we were in Hell
"Goddamn they're back,!" I screamed inside my head. "Filthy little
motherfuckers! "

Worms.

The human kind.

They woke me up from a tomb sleep itching my ass like it was on
fire. I checked: no worms. A blood-red hemorrhoid.

But I knew all about worms. A couple pounds of them fell out of me
in Vietnam. Each the obscene same. Coprophiliacs.

& if you wonder why I sleep alone

don't.

The clock needed cleaning
Out of the corner of his eye

he saw the shadows rushing him. A black flash to his immediate right, another coming from the left. No no no no, they can't be Viet Cong, he told himself, not now, not in 1992, can't be, cannot be. He closed his eyes & fully expected to feel a knife punch through his head.

He opened them slowly, breathing in quick draws of air hysterically as a pair of black pajamas opened at his feet.

One heart left

one body.

✦ ✦ ✦

A five line story
It was early evening when the phone rang; I got it.
"Bill?" she asked. "Bill Shields?"
I couldn't place the voice. "Are you still alive?" she continued.
There was nothing to say.
The phone fell asleep.

✦ ✦ ✦

skating like a turd on ice
The first thirty years were such a bad joke - himself, the women, the lies, parents, & old cars - all of 'em drunk & passed out on the floor. Children fell like the very rain & he was drenched to the bone.

He was walking away from people, even when he was right in the middle of their sexual organ. Temporary, everyone temporary...

No regrets; people were lined up to sit in his back seat.

& then he turned thirty-one & people started to die in his life.

Those next ten years were worse.

They lasted.

+ + +

payday
After 46 days of a VA hospital bed, he left with a hundred percent
disability check for the month, a government pen, & a bottle of pills.
The taxi let him off at the foot of the bridge - that check hadn't been
cashed yet.-

The railing was knee-high; the drop was a hundred foot to the rocks
& water clear enough to see the Coke bottles thrown from cars long
ago. He remembered throwing a few himself.

Goddamn medicine, he thought as he started walking, VA bastards
& their damn pills. He rested a hand on the railing, going to his
knees, the sweat pouring down his nose.

The bridge held his name on its metal lips

c'mon. it's only a few feet

there's plenty of water to catch you

He leaned in, looked straight down at the rocks, & yelled, "I'll be
back, you son of a bitch!

soon as I cash my check."

+ + +

A travel brochure
1. The sound of the night train.
2. An empty pair of shoes next to the rails.
3. No one answers the pay phone.

✦ ✦ ✦

The velocity of sadness
The pistol became an extension of his head.

Evenings were a spin of the chamber & the ritual of loading well greased rounds into six holes. A wipe of the barrel with a chamois. He read the manufacturer's name a thousand times on the barrel. Ruger.

Quick - he puts the gun up to his temple, desperately thinking of one damn good reason not to kill himself. One damn good reason.

No one would be at his funeral.

The gun goes down

maybe.

✦ ✦ ✦

going Greyhound
At exactly the same moment I fell asleep, my ex-wife in Minnesota was giving head to her boyfriend; my littlest daughter was on the pot; my oldest was sleeping, dreaming of colleges & men. Our cat was pulling the rug out from under its claws; the dog was in the neighbor's garbage. 3 radios were on.

I woke up, had a cigarette & a swallow of coffee.

Later, I went back to Vietnam with the family

& we ate the dog.

✦ ✦ ✦

A cute little ditty

The man laid in bed late into the morning, thinking about his never seen son, & wished him dead.

The kid was a thousand miles away & never thought about his father.

Mama's little lovers ...

hate mama.

+ + +
brown paperbag childhoods
The kids spent more time finding her bottles & draining them down sinks than she ever spent drinking. After school, they combed the house for the fifths. After work, she walked the house like a tomb, shaking the cupboards for an ounce of alcohol.

It went on like that for years. One kid left home at nineteen; another one never finished high school & joined the Navy. Eventually, even the baby left for drier pastures.

She never stopped hiding those bottles, as if they were pearls falling into unworthy hands.

Pearls big enough to eat a body.

She ate good.

+ + +
A micro Story
It was a simple enough request, & loaded with lawyers and monthly checks.

"Please turn out that light," she asked, & he smashed the lamp to the floor.

They had no more children.

Their house disappeared.

The baby died.

+ + +

The wail of anonymity
Stripped to his waist

he slammed a broomstick against the ceiling, screaming as he went, "Turn that goddamn television down!" & the old lady upstairs never heard him. Every night the same - an incredibly loud tv turned to game shows & local news - & the numerous flushes of the toilet. He knew her habits as well as she - he just hated her more.

They never saw each other's face.

But they lived together

bed bug style.

+ + +

a Walt Whitman symphony for the damned

He thought he was the loneliest man alive. & while waiting in the car for his wife at the drug store, he pulled out the clutch & drove the Plymouth right off the earth. There were 5,937,002 people in America lonelier than him that day:

8/15/92.

WONDERFUL GHOST STORY

A Hard Dead Man
I'll be crawling between my woman's thighs - really just getting there, on two knees & balancing myself on one hand as I insert myself w/the other - not thinking at all, my mind on one simple thing, when the old man will shift his weight in the bed, groan w/the effort of pulling himself to the edge; his white goatee fairly glows against the sheet. I don't know his name. I killed him in Vietnam, we've been close since.

"Pretty good, boy, now take your time not like last time," he says, watching me intently.

"Okay" I nod back at him.

My woman sighs.

I've never told her about the old man, hell no she wouldn't understand. I don't either, completely.

She sighs once more.

I grunt.

The old man flashes me: THUMB DOWN.

Fuck that old man.

● ■ ■ ◉

Light as a Feather, Dead as a Doorknob
When I wake up & walk out to the livingroom, she wakes up on the couch w/her baby & goes back to the bedroom. The day she died, her entire village died. She's been toting that baby to her breast for at least twenty years - jesus christ, I've looked at her Buddhist face for

twenty years. I wish she'd change her clothes.

I saw her blown apart one afternoon, the baby in her arms. I didn't kill her.

That baby is starting to look a little like me.

A blonde-haired Vietnamese baby.

The couch is still warm from their sleep. I sip coffee on their footprints.

❀ ◼ ◼ ❀

Blow out the Candles Honey, We're Coming Home
She can't be more than seven years old & I've never seen her smile. Seriously she hooks up her seat belt in my car & watches the road.

I hope she likes this Plymouth; I know she liked my truck. She could put her feet on the dashboard & shift her butt around.

The napalm must've really gotten her bad. Her one arm & leg are scarred totally. Her right ear was burned off. She was just one more kid out of a million dead children who died somewhere in Southeast Asia.

She taps her good leg impatiently when I'm tailgating the asshole in front of me.

Damn, that child really gets on my nerves.

❀ ◼ ◼ ❀

The Whirring of Metal, The Sound of Wings
"Funny, eh boy," said the old man, pointing to the apartment parking lot. He had tied up the mutilated carcasses of a hundred water buffalo to all the cars; most definitely bizarre, a new Ford Thunderbird had the tongue of a water buffalo sticking on its windshield.

God only knows where he dragged those poor beasts from - looked like a mini-gun or a good Huey gunner just mowed 'em down.

It smelled like they'd been dead a long, long time, just like the neighbors.

The birds fell on the meat like the very rain.

● ■ ■ ●

You Don't Love Me Yet

She startled me, I caught myself from falling in the shower; 6:30 a.m. & I didn't have the light on in the bathroom, enjoying the black air & warm water. I heard the baby making sucking sounds against her chest. She was in there w/me.

I handed her a washcloth.

She turned her back to me, her hair running to the top of her torn pajamas. There are holes there where the bullets pinned her to the mud.

The baby isn't a pretty sight; his face is untouched but an M-16 bullet tore the back & legs right out of him.

I've never heard him cry.

● ■ ■ ●

A Dead Viet Cong Shakes the Buddha's Hand

I was eating Salisbury steak; the old man liked his chowder. We sat at an old scarred table eating supper & looking out the window, watching the snow.

"I gotta get you a woman," I said, chewing on that fancy burger.

He nodded no.

"I watch you enough," he said.

& we laughed.

The night turned black & the snow came thru the street lights, we shared a cigarette. I thought about the night I killed him, we never discuss it. Dead is dead in this house.

Just ask the damn ghosts.

● ▨ ▨ ●

A Tiny Bee Spinning in my Ear
Two old ladies playing Scrabble on my livingroom floor never feel my foot go right thru 'em & out the other side; the game goes on, their shrill voices fighting over words.

I shut the lights off. It's a token gesture. Neither one has eyes to see with.

These old women are composites of every old woman I saw broken in pieces, lying face down in Vietnamese mud, dead on the doorstep of a hootch. They are some tough old buzzards.

& it's my name they're spelling over & over on that cheezy board; Bill Sheilds/Bill Sihelds/Bill Seilds/Bill Sheisd/Bill Bill Bill...

It's I before E, ladies.

● ▨ ▨ ●

We Called for Help but the Line was Busy
The old man was walking me thru a bad nightmare of Vietnam; I had my arm around his shoulder & we walked around the apartment. He took my gun away. For later.

"Go back in there, boy," he said, "that woman make you forget all about us dead Viet Cong."

I shook my head.

"I dream of you Americans too," he said. The six inch hairs on his chin never moved.

It was a tender moment, Hallmark cards were smacking their lips. I fell asleep on his bullet wound.

He doesn't sleep, the liar.

● ■ ■ ●

10,000 Howling Wolves

I have a room full of dead Amerasian babies, floor-to-ceiling kids, all color combinations & religions. Some never even saw Vietnam; they died inside their mother. We have the B-52 shelf w/unrecognizable children. A napalm shelf, an artillery round shelf etc. I've done my best to keep them dusted, organized. A library, of sorts, of parts.

People dance in that room. There's this terrific sense of well-being in a room full of dead babies. It gives one rhythm, a spark to the step. My woman keeps her stereo in there & she dances by herself to an ancient Grateful Dead song.

I don't think it's much - just a bunch of dead babies.

● ■ ■ ●

A Cold Night for Dogs

I was on my back, looking at the ceiling above the bed. My woman was turned on her side, the blanket wrapped around her mummy like.

"Okay, boy," the old man said, gesturing to me w/his pinky finger, the four inch fingernail curling slightly up. He wanted me to look at the eyes that were glowing in the closet, a few eyeballs glared back at the foot of the bed.

"My friends," he added. "They VC too."

I made some room on the bed & the whole platoon came crawling in, leaving their weapons on the floor. They slept like the living.

It was a cold night for alligators.

◉ ▨ ▨ ◉

GOTHIC

1.

A dirty green house too far from the road. More than a few garbage bags of beer cans on the lawn, the weeds 2 feet high. Wooden shutters perched against the house.

Inside. Old woman's bag of clothes, full ashtrays, fist size holes in the sofa, burn marks on the kitchen table. A bed stained with menstrual blood.

Picture of a haloed Jesus in the bathroom, right above the toilet.

The rush of roaches. Mice in the garbage; silverfish in the sink.

Home.

2.

My mother is dead, my father too. Wait. They might be alive, maybe I've thought they were dead for so long, they died. Or I did.

So full of lies...

3.

I'm lost in stories. The truth is an accident willing to expire. I can't remember, was Vietnam a dream, something I saw in my sleep? I don't know. It feels real but.

The name <u>Bill</u> <u>Shields</u> is a dead man's handle; I broke my own name off, with my social security number, & pitched it into the garbage.

Sears gave me a credit card; I'm made-up man, perfect for credit.

4.
Stroke your sick mother's face when she's this sick. You'd rather be in a car with the windows down, listening to a heart, not an old, embarrassing woman.

"& while you're down there, bring me a glass of tea, p-l-e-a-s-e honey," she asks.

& you get it. Bring it to the bedside.

"I'll be right downstairs if you need anything, Mom."

Walk right out the fucking door.

5.
My death would be okay if I could come back in 2 weeks with a full billfold.

6.
I listen to the boss attentively. I sir him; I give him a strong 8 hours. No lip, I'll work over, sir.

I hate the man, think of screwdrivers pounded into his eyes; his kids born deformed; his mother raped in front of him, repeatedly.

I'm his man.

Just ask him.

7.
Bodies in bags piled against the wall. Olive-drab bags, the bodies slurping when I move them.

Whole people, or mostly, inside. Teeth inhaled into guts, a head by a kneecap, vertebrae wrapped around a torso like hanging rope. Some blackish blood pooled in the seams.

We couldn't get it all out of Vietnam.

8.
Every morning is the same melancholy of sick assholes shitting in my mind; I try to forget but the rage... I could kill before 8:00 a.m.

9.
No lies in a sealed coffin.

I think too much about death & nothing about dying. Like everyone else, I want my ass around for forever - with as little pain as needed.

I don't want to die with my wife; I'll let her go first.

Even my daughters can die before me, I'm selfish.

It ain't the dying

it's the living

I can't work out.

10.
She stared right at me, grey eyes looking at brown.

"Daddy, where <u>were</u> you?"

"Out, honey, just out."

11.
Even after we slept together once, she called me David. David, was it good for you, honey? Right there, David. David, how's your day going? You were married before, weren't you David?

I liked the name. Maybe dye my hair brown, wear clean corduroys. Take the McDonald's sacks out of my car.

I could be David.

12.

Cheese pizza, no meat, no mushrooms. Yards of pizza dripping with sauce around the body.

She was still alive - I had to look more than hard - eyes closed, hands blue & limp, sucking air with the nothing she had left.

A dying coach was with her. An old lady too, slice of pizza in her hand. Plus. All this damn woman's friends sitting around here, eating & gabbing.

No. This had to be a dream, not right here, in front of me. I stayed long enough to buy auto parts.

13.

She lit a joint & dropped her cat off the porch, 2 floors down.

"Blacky likes it," she said. I stared down into the bushes. That cat wasn't moving, a clump of fur looked to be speared into a shrub.

She forgot about him. & I left late that night, never saw her again. The cat liked it. My ass.

14.

"You know, Bill, nobody knows you, down deep. Like your secrets, doesn't anybody know the total you?" she asked, lighting a Benson & Hedges mild.

I don't answer some questions. Like that one.

The tv has & had more answers than my skull. Who cares? We give 'em what we want.

"Bastard," she hissed & ground out the butt. "Fucking bastard with his secrets."

Yep, she ain't paid for the whole bloody show.

15.

I never felt like killing a woman after sex but... I could always kill myself.

That bad sadness after the gland squeezes & the bed soaks up the juice. The horror of facing yourself again with every thought of self-loathing. Who knows why, it just is.

I can love the woman & hate myself... bad movies of me playing at the cinema of dirt. Tickets 2 Off after 9 p.m.

Popcorn poured over bones.

16.

I don't call old friends. They're better off in my imagination, naked or drunk, or witty as hell.

No one needs a 2 a.m. call from me & I don't want to hear their life's boredom.

My number is unlisted just in case someone has a wild hair

up their finger.

17.

I've punished myself & lived in rooms no bigger than freezer cartons. Ten of us living in a space no bigger than an efficiency apartment.

I needed to be alone, forgotten especially to myself; I dreamt only of corpses. In the morning, I made strong coffee & sat alone.

Every man & woman I ever abused walked into that room.

I apologized to short, green walls.

18.
I've been hung too long, addicted to pain for the shame... watched my mother die with a bottle tucked in tight next to her bed. I felt more comfortable in Vietnam, the killing, the killed.

I've got to go now. Say my goodbyes. Goodbye.